MEAT

FOR GROWING CHRISTIANS

Frank Hamrick & Jerry Dean

PositiveAction
BIBLE CURRICULUM

MEAT: FOR GROWING CHRISTIANS
written by Frank Hamrick and Jerry Dean

Copyright 1972, 1973, 1993, 2008, 2013 by Positive Action for Christ, Inc.,
P.O. Box 700, 502 W. Pippen St., Whitakers, NC 27891.

www.positiveaction.org

5th edition 2013
First printing

Printed in the United States of America

ISBN: 978-1-59557-171-7

Edited by C.J. Harris and Jim Lord
Designed by Shannon Brown

Published by

PositiveAction
BIBLE CURRICULUM

TABLE OF CONTENTS

But strong meat belongeth to them that are of full age, even those who by reason of use have their senses exercised to discern both good and evil.

—Hebrews 5:14

The verse above literally means "solid food belongs to the fully trained athlete who, because of practice, has his senses trained to discern good and evil." Do you want to become that fully trained athlete? Do you want to run the race that He has called you to? Then *Meat* is for you.

Infants don't start out eating solid food, but as they grow and mature, they learn to appreciate meat. Are you ready to begin your *Meat* diet? Sometimes it will be tough. Often it will be hard to digest. You will have to spend much time in order to get all the good things from *Meat*. But, if you stay with it to the end, you will realize that your spiritual strength has increased more and more with each meal.

If you're ready to begin, pray right now and ask the Lord to teach you by His Spirit, causing you to become that fully trained athlete for Him.

1

THE INSPIRATION
OF THE BIBLE:
BIBLIOLOGY

That is a question people ask frequently. In fact, some of your unsaved friends probably have already asked you that question. Even some pastors in liberal churches don't think the Bible is inspired.

DEFINITION OF INSPIRATION

Inspiration means God-breathed. When used in connection with the Scriptures, it means that God breathed into the minds of the writers exactly what He wanted them to say.

I've been inspired by a beautiful view before.

That's one type of inspiration, but that's not the same type of inspiration that we have in mind.

TWO TYPES OF INSPIRATION

Natural Inspiration

This is inspiration on the human level—the kind caused by psychological and environmental influences on an individual. For instance, due to certain moods and events in one's life, we have various impulses to draw a picture, write a poem, compose a song, play ball, etc. This is not what we mean by biblical inspiration.

Biblical Inspiration

This is inspiration on the heavenly level—the kind caused by God Himself breathing into people the actual words He wants them to write. This was purely for the purpose of revelation. God has finished this type of inspiration.

Is God still inspiring people to write?

GOD HAS STOPPED INSPIRING PEOPLE TO WRITE THE WORD OF GOD

In the last book of the Bible, God had John write a warning. What was it? (Rev. 22:18) _____

_____

_____

You can rest assured that all of God's Word has been revealed by Him. The Book is finished—it cannot be added to or taken away from. Yet Satan continues to attack at this very point.

SATAN ATTACKS THE INSPIRATION OF GOD'S WORD

Ask yourself a couple of simple questions:

1. If the Bible is not completely true in every detail, can we know for sure that we are saved? _____

2. Can we trust any part of the Bible if it is incorrect in certain places? _____

If the Bible is not God's Word, then we are poor, ignorant individuals who can know nothing about the life that Christ has to offer. Isn't it logical that the first thing the devil will attack is the truthfulness and trustworthiness of God's Word? _____

> How can I defeat these attacks on God's Word?

DEFEATING SATAN'S ATTACKS ON THE WORD OF GOD

No Errors

First, we need to know that the Bible contains no error in its archaeological, scientific, geographic, or historical record. Even though it was written many years before people knew all they know today, it does not contain even one error. Could a book be written by a group of men over different periods of time, about subjects that these men were not experts in, and still be without any error in archaeology, science, history, etc.? _____

There is only one logical way for this to happen: A supernatural power must have directed its writing! If it is not humanly possible for such a book to be written, then a Being who knows everything there is to know must have written the book. Who, then, must have written the Scriptures? _____

Let's look at a second reason why we can be sure the Bible is God's Word.

Fulfilled Prophecy

Second, what about fulfilled prophecies? Everything the Bible has said would happen has happened exactly as prophesied. The Old Testament was written hundreds of years before Christ, and many things were written about Christ even before He was born. Read these verses and tell what was written about Christ many years before He came to Earth. Write the answers on the longer lines.

_____ 1. Psalm 16:8–11 _____
_____

_____ 2. Psalm 22:16 _____
_____

_____ 3. Psalm 22:18 _____
_____

_____ 4. Psalm 34:20 _____
_____

_____ 5. Psalm 41:9 _____
_____

_____ 6. Psalm 68:18 _____
_____

_____ 7. Psalm 69:21 _____

_____

_____ 8. Psalm 110:1 _____

_____

_____ 9. Isaiah 7:14 _____

_____

_____ 10. Micah 5:2 _____

_____

_____ 11. Zechariah 9:9 _____

_____

_____ 12. Zechariah 11:12–13 _____

_____

The following verses record how each of the previous prophecies were fulfilled. Now match the following verses, placing the letter of the correct passage below on the appropriate line on the shorter lines above.

A. John 19:31–33   G. Matthew 2:6

B. Matthew 26:15; 27:9–10   H. John 13:18

C. Matthew 1:23   I. Colossians 3:1

D. Matthew 27:34   J. Ephesians 4:7–8

E. Matthew 21:1–6   K. Acts 2:23–27

F. John 20:20, 25   L. Matthew 27:35

- Could all of these prophecies have been fulfilled perfectly if God's Word were not true?_____

It would be incredibly unlikely—perhaps even impossible—for all of the above prophecies to have come true by accident. Yet there are literally hundreds of prophecies in God's Word, all of which came true, exactly as God said. No single person, much less a group of people over hundreds of years, could have devised a set of prophecies so accurate. God's Word is not human, but supernatural.

The Bible's Own Testimony

Third, let's look at what the Bible itself says about the Word of God.

In the Old Testament alone, the phrase "thus saith the Lord" occurs more than 3,800 times. Read these verses and explain in your own words what they mean.

- 2 Peter 1:19–21 _____

  _____

  _____

- 2 Timothy 3:16 _____

  _____

  _____

- By these two verses we can see that God used men to write His Word. However, these men were taught, or *moved*, by what? _____

- According to 2 Timothy 3:16, how much Scripture is true? _____

Christ's Own Testimony

What did Jesus Himself say about the Word?

- Matthew 5:18_____

  _____

- Luke 16:17 _____

  _____

- John 10:34–35 _____

  _____

Read these statements carefully. If one is true, put a check beside it; if it is false, put an X beside it and state why it is false.

_____ The Bible contains the Word of God. _____

_____

_____ When you read the Bible, it becomes the Word of God to you. _____

_____

_____ All Scripture that is given by inspiration of God is profitable. _____

_____

_____ The Bible is all the Word of God, and every single word is completely true and trustworthy. _____

_____

Complete This Section Without Looking Back at the Lesson

1. What does the word *inspiration* mean when it refers to the Bible?_____

   _____

   _____

2. Name the two types of inspiration: _____

   _____

   _____

3. Name four ways we can *know* God's Word is inspired:

   _____

   _____

   _____

   _____

Verses to Memorize

- 2 Peter 1:20–21
- 2 Timothy 3:16

2
JESUS CHRIST: CHRISTOLOGY

We have just seen that the Bible is completely true and reliable on every subject it addresses. There is much talk today about one such subject—Jesus. But are all the things people say about Him true? Is Christ just a good teacher or a prophet, or is He more? Was He just a good man, or was He God in the flesh? Let's see what the Bible says.

> *He's the Lord: God in the flesh.*

WHAT GOD'S WORD SAYS

- Read John 1:1–2, 14 and 1 John 1:1. Who is the Word mentioned in these verses? _____

- How long had this Word existed? _____

- Then, we could safely say that Jesus Christ is _____
  _____

- John 1:1–2 states that Christ was already in existence in the beginning with God, but then it adds that the Word was _____
  _____

- Read Colossians 1:16–17; John 1:3; Ephesians 3:9; and Hebrews 1:1–3. According to these verses, what did Christ do? And what does He continue to do? _____
  _____
  _____

- These verses show that Christ is _____

- If Christ were only a good teacher or prophet, would He be eternal? _____

- Could He have actually created the universe? _____

WHAT CHRIST SAID

- Notice what Christ said about Himself. Read John 10:30; 14:8–9. In your own words, state what Jesus said about Himself. _____

  _____

  _____

HIS NAMES PROVE HIS DEITY

Match the names of Christ with the Scripture references.

	1. John 1:29	A. The Messiah
	2. John 1:34	B. The Good Shepherd
	3. John 1:41	C. The Lamb of God
	4. John 1:49	D. The Bread of Life
	5. John 6:48	E. The Son of God; Holy One of God
	6. John 6:69	F. The Door/Gate of the Sheep
	7. John 8:12; 9:5	G. The Resurrection and the Life
	8. John 10:7–8	H. The Son of God; His Chosen One
	9. John 10:11	I. The Way, Truth, and Life
	10. John 11:25	J. The Son of God, King of Israel
	11. John 14:6	K. The Light of the World
	12. John 15:1	L. The True Vine
	13. John 20:27–29	M. Lord and God
	14. Revelation 1:8	N. Alpha and Omega, The Almighty

HE IS EITHER GOD OR A LIAR

Many say that Christ was not God, that He was not the Savior of the world, but He might have been great teacher or leader or a good man. But if Christ was not God, as He claimed to be, then He was a liar or insane. If Jesus Christ is not God, He couldn't have been a good man.

OTHER FACTS THAT PROVE CHRIST'S DEITY

We will now look at several other facts that prove Christ was God in the flesh. Look up these verses and state those things that prove Christ was God.

- Isaiah 7:14; Matthew 1:18; Luke 1:26–27

  _____
  _____

- 1 John 3:5; 2 Corinthians 5:21; Hebrews 4:15

  _____
  _____

- John 20:1–8, 19, 26; 1 Corinthians 15:3–8

  _____
  _____

- Ancient Jewish law required two witnesses to establish something as true. In modern societies, the legal standards are largely the same, given enough evidence. How many people saw Christ alive after His resurrection?

  _____
  _____

Complete This Section Without Looking Back at the Lesson

1. List the facts as well as the Scriptures that prove to your satisfaction that Christ was truly God. _____

   _____
   _____
   _____
   _____
   _____

_____

_____

_____

2. Could Christ not be God and still be a good man?

_____

3. Prove your answer. _____

_____

_____

_____

_____

_____

_____

_____

Verses to Memorize

- John 20:28–29

3

THE TRINITY: THEOLOGY

You have probably heard a preacher or someone else talk about "the Holy Trinity." Perhaps also you have some vague idea of what is meant by the word *Trinity*. The classic definition of the Trinity is this: "The three eternal distinctions in one divine essence, known as the Father, the Son, and the Holy Spirit."

> ### *What does that mean?*

It simply means that even though God is only one Being, or essence, this one Being exists in three separate persons: the Father, Son, and Holy Spirit.

> ### *That's hard to believe. I could never explain that.*

I can't explain it either. Though if we could figure out God, He wouldn't be much of a God, would He? But we can offer proof that there is a Holy Trinity—however mysterious or confusing the concept might be.

PROOF OF THE TRINITY

Let's see what the Bible says about this subject.

The Bible Constantly Associates the Three Together in Their Work

1. Read Romans 1:7; Galatians 1:1; Ephesians 1:2. In each of these verses what two persons are connected together?
   God the _____
   and _____

2. All three are mentioned at the baptism of Jesus. Note Matthew 3:16–17. How does this passage portray each member of the Trinity?

   • The Father_____
   _____

- The Son _____

  _____

- The Holy Spirit _____

  _____

3. According to Matthew 28:19, in whose name were the disciples to baptize? _____

4. A blessing from the Apostle Paul unites the three. Read 2 Corinthians 13:14 and write the verse below:

   _____

   _____

   _____

   _____

   _____

5. All three are united in our salvation. Read 1 Peter 1:2 and state what part each plays in our salvation.

   - The Father _____

     _____

   - The Son _____

     _____

   - The Holy Spirit _____

     _____

   - To summarize, all three are associated and united in at least four ways:
     - The baptism of Jesus
     - The baptism of believers
     - Paul's blessing on the church
     - Salvation

6. All three take part in our spiritual growth. Read 2 Corinthians 3:12–18 and summarize verses 17–18 in your own words. _____

_____

_____

_____

Their Eternal Existence Proves the Trinity

1. According to Psalm 90:2, how long has God the Father existed? _____

2. What does the Bible say about the Spirit's life-span? (Heb. 9:14)_____

_____

3. What does John 1:1–2 say about God the Son? _____

_____

Creation Proves the Trinity

1. Read Genesis 1:26. Notice the two pronouns that refer to God used in the verse: _____ and _____. Are these singular or plural?_____

   • What does this tell you about God? _____

   _____

2. Now, look at John 1:1–3, 14. Who else aided in creation?

   _____

   • John 1:34 tells us that this other person is called what?

   _____

3. Go back to Genesis 1:2. Who moved over the waters before creation?_____

What difference does it make if I believe in the Trinity or not?

The Trustworthiness of Christ

1. Read John 14:7–12. In verse 9, Christ says that anyone who has seen Him has also seen _____.

2. And in John 10:30, Jesus says _____
    _____

3. Therefore, if we reject the doctrine of the Trinity, we say that _____ is a liar, and cannot be trusted.

Our Faith in the Truthfulness of God's Word

1. Read 2 Peter 1:20–21. Who wrote the words of God?
    _____

    •   According to verse 21, who moved these men as they wrote Scripture? _____

2. Therefore, if we reject the Trinity, we deny the fact that God wrote the Word. Could we then know for sure that the Bible was true in every detail? _____

The Assurance of Our Salvation

1. Read 1 John 3:24; 4:13; and Romans 8:14, 16. State in your own words what these verses mean._____
    _____
    _____
    _____
    _____

2. If we reject the Trinity, can we be sure we're saved? ___

The Enlightening Power of the Spirit

•   Read John 14:26; 15:26. According to these verses, what work does the Comforter, the Holy Spirit, perform?
    _____
    _____
    _____

- However, if He is not God, can He honestly tell us the mind of God? _____

- Then, if we deny the doctrine of the Trinity, can we really understand the Scriptures? _____

BRIEF SUMMARY

The doctrine of the Trinity, simply stated, is that the Holy Spirit is God, Jesus Christ is God, and God the Father is God. They are all three separate, yet they are one God.

Complete This Section Without Looking Back at the Lesson

1. Give the simple definition of the Trinity. _____
   _____
   _____

2. Name three major proofs of the Trinity. _____
   _____
   _____
   _____

3. Name four ways the Bible associates the Three-in-One.
   _____
   _____
   _____
   _____

4. Who created the heavens and the earth and everything in them? Be specific. _____
   _____

5. What four great truths must we discard if we reject the doctrine of the Trinity? _____
   _____
   _____
   _____

Verses to Memorize

- 2 Corinthians 13:14
- John 1:1–4

4

THE HOLY SPIRIT: PNEUMATOLOGY

We have already seen in an earlier section that the Holy Spirit is a part of the Trinity—He is God. There is a great deal of emphasis placed upon the Holy Spirit today, but not everything taught about Him is true. In this chapter we will see what the Bible says about the person and work of the Holy Spirit.

> *Who is the Holy Spirit?*

HIS PERSON

The first thing we must understand is that the Holy Spirit is a person, just as Christ and God the Father are persons.

> *How can a Spirit be a Person?*

Personality is determined by the possession of . . .

- Intellect—the ability to think and express thought
- Emotion—the ability to have feelings
- Will—the ability to make decisions and act upon them

- Look at the following verses: Ephesians 4:30; 1 Corinthians 2:10–11; Acts 13:2; and 1 Corinthians 12:11. Which of these verses states that the Spirit has . . .

  - Intellect _____

  - Emotion _____

  - Will _____

- Proof that the Holy Spirit is a person can be easily found in that the Spirit is never referred to as *it*. The correct translation should be *He*. Read John 16:13–15. How many times is the word *He* used in referring to the Holy Spirit? _____

> *What does the Holy Spirit do?*

HIS WORK

Now, let us look at the actual work of the Holy Spirit in conversion. There are four words in the New Testament which indicate the Holy Spirit's work *during* and *after* conversion.

Birth

- You may remember a verse in the *Milk* booklet stating that all who receive Christ become children of God. Read John 1:12–13 again.

- How do we become actual children in a family on Earth?
  _____
  _____

- How do you think we are able to become children of God? _____
  _____

- Look at John 3:3. What did Jesus tell Nicodemus was necessary for him to see the kingdom of God? _____
  _____

- In verse 5, what two things did Jesus say we must be born of? _____
  _____

- Verse 6 explains verse 5. The first birth or natural birth is a "water birth" because each child spends nine months in the mother's womb. What then, do the two words in verse 5 mean, as explained in verse 6?

  - Water _____
    _____

  - Spirit _____
    _____

- We see that we are sons of God because we have been _____ of the Spirit.

Baptism

- Read 1 Corinthians 12:12–13. These verses tell us that we are all _____ into one body by the Spirit. The word *baptism* means to submerge, to place into.

> ### What does it mean to be baptized into one body?

Read carefully Romans 12:4–5; Ephesians 1:19–23; 4:4; 5:23, 30, 32 and Colossians 1:18, and answer the following questions.

- Who is the "head" spoken of in these verses? _____
  _____

- What is the "body" spoken of in these verses? _____
  _____

- What is the "church"? _____
  _____

- How many people have been baptized, or placed, into this body? _____

- Now, read 1 Corinthians 12:12–13 again very carefully. State in your own words what it means to be baptized into one body by the Spirit. _____
  _____
  _____
  _____
  _____

Indwelling

- Read Romans 8:9, 11 and 1 Corinthians 3:16; 6:19–20. According to these verses, where does the Holy Spirit live? _____
  _____

- So according to 1 Corinthians 6:19–20, what is your body? _____
  _____

- Does your body belong to yourself? _____

- Then, to whom does it belong? _____

- In light of this, how is a Christian to live? Be specific.
  _____
  _____
  _____

Filling

- The fourth word we want to consider concerning the work of the Holy Spirit is found in Ephesians 5:18. Here we are commanded to be _____ with the Holy Spirit.

The word *filled* means to be controlled by the Spirit. A literal translation of this verse could read, "Be constantly, moment by moment, controlled by the Holy Spirit."

- Let's look again at the four words that describe the Holy Spirit's work. List them.

  1. _____

  2. _____

  3. _____

  4. _____

- If we are born by the Spirit, can we ever be any less born into God's family? _____

- If we are baptized into the body of Christ, which is the Church, can we ever become more baptized? _____

- The baptism of the Spirit occurs _____ time. What happens at this moment? (Eph. 1:13-14)

  _____

- If the Holy Spirit lives in us, will He ever leave us? (Heb. 13:5; Matt. 28:20) _____

- However, a Christian who is filled can still try to ignore the influence of the Spirit. How?_____

  _____

In other words, we always have all of Him, but we don't always let Him control all of us. Do you live a life in submission to the Holy Spirit? What areas of your life have you not yielded to Him?

_____

- Finally, let's see how we can resist the Holy Spirit—so we can avoid it. Read Acts 2:1–4. When the Holy Spirit first came upon the Christians, in what form did He come? (v. 3)

  _____

- Now read 1 Thessalonians 5:19. What are we told not to do to the Holy Spirit? _____

- In your own life, how have you quenched or put out— like water on a flame—the Holy Spirit's work in your life?

  _____

  _____

- Read Ephesians 4:30. What must we not do?

  _____

- Since the Holy Spirit is a real person, He can be grieved. You can grieve Him as you would grieve your mother or father. Read Ephesians 4:25–32 and list the things that grieve the Holy Spirit. _____

  _____

  _____

  _____

Christian, examine your heart. Does the Holy Spirit fill you? Does He control every area of your entire life? Or has His work been quenched, His person grieved by your rebellion against Him?

Complete This Section Without Looking Back at the Lesson

1. List at least two verses that present the Holy Spirit as a person. _____

_____

2. Are we ever correct to refer to the Holy Spirit as "it"? _____ Why? _____

_____

_____

3. List four words that describe the work of the Holy Spirit and describe what each means.

- _____

_____

- _____

_____

- _____

_____

- _____

_____

4. When is a person born of the Spirit? _____

_____

5. When is a person baptized by the Spirit? _____

_____

6. When is a person indwelled by the Spirit? _____

_____

7. When is a person filled with the Spirit? _____

_____

Verses to Memorize

- Ephesians 5:18
- Ephesians 4:30
- 1 Corinthians 6:19–20

5
MANKIND: ANTHROPOLOGY

"People are essentially good. Each person possesses a spark of divinity which can be fanned into flames of goodness by the proper environment. To improve ourselves, we must first improve our education and living conditions."

You have probably heard this statement. Maybe you haven't heard it quite that way, but you have no doubt something similar. These statements reflect an idealized view of mankind, but the Bible presents a different picture. In this chapter, we are going to see exactly what the Bible says concerning our nature.

ADAM AND EVE

A Perfect Environment

- When God created the world, He made a beautiful garden, Eden—the perfect environment. Read Genesis 1:1–25. Pay special attention to verses 10, 12, 18, 21, and 25. What one phrase occurs in all these verses?

  _____

A Perfect Man

- And in this perfect environment, God made Adam. Read Genesis 1:26–27 and 2:7. What do we learn about Adam from these verses? _____

  _____

  _____

A Perfect Woman

- Genesis also tells us about Eve's creation. God did not want Adam to be alone, so He created Eve using Adam's own body. According to verse 24, God brought this first man and woman together so that they could be

  _____.

- Notice also one thing God told Adam to do in the garden. Genesis 2:15. _____

- Read Genesis 2:16–17 and state the one thing Adam was forbidden to do. _____

  _____

- According to verse 17, what was his punishment if he broke God's commandment? _____

ADAM'S SIN AND ITS EFFECTS

You probably know what happened in Genesis 3. Adam and Eve were tempted by Satan and broke God's commandment. Now note the effects of Adam's sin.

It Affected Mankind's Relationship to God

- How did Adam's sin affect mankind's relationship to God? (Gen. 3:23–24)_____

  _____

It Affected Mankind's Perfectly-Created Nature

- Adam and Eve once walked in fellowship with God, unashamed. Now what did they try to do? (Gen. 3:8–10) _____

  _____

It Affected Mankind Physically

- How did it affect mankind physically? (Gen. 3:19; Rom. 5:12; and 1 Cor. 15:22) _____

  _____

  _____

  _____

- How did it affect the environment in which mankind lived? (Gen. 3:14, 17–19)_____

_____

_____

_____

You may think, "But I didn't sin in the garden! Why do I suffer because of something my ancestors did so long ago?"

- What tragic results sin brought upon man. We don't know everything that happened as a result of Adam's disobedience, but we do know that every person since Adam has been under God's condemnation. Read Romans 5:12–21. In these verses there is a parallel drawn between what two people? _____

- Keep that parallel in mind. Read Romans 5:14 and explain in your own words the role Adam played in relation to Christ—the one who was to come.

_____

_____

_____

- According to verse 12, what two things entered the world by one man? _____ and _____.

- Now, read verses 17–19. According to verse 19, what happened because of one man's disobedience?_____

_____

And because of one Man's obedience? _____

_____

Adam was the world's first unrighteous man and passed his death to us. Christ, being God, came and lived as the world's first righteous man and gave His life for us.

- Read the following Scriptures and state in your own words mankind's condition before God (Rom. 3:9–19, 23; Rom. 7:18; Isa. 1:4–6; 53:6; Jer. 17:9).

  _____

  _____

  _____

THE ANSWER TO MANKIND'S PROBLEMS

- People today are making great efforts to cure the problems of the world. Poverty, war, sickness, and drug abuse can all be eliminated by better education, better housing, or more money, they say. But is mankind's real problem an outward or an inward deficiency? _____

- According to the Bible, what is the one basic cause of all mankind's problems? _____

- Is this an outward or an inward problem? _____

- Can it be cured outwardly or inwardly? _____

- What is the first step that needs to be taken to solve man's problems? _____

- What is the only cure for sin? _____

- Thus, the real cure for the problems of man is _____

  _____

Remember: Peace cannot come without Christ. Peace must be achieved inwardly. The cessation of war won't bring peace. Man must stop war with God by receiving Christ as his Lord and Savior before he will ever realize inward peace.

1. Name the four areas affected by Adam's sin.

    _____

    _____

    _____

    _____

2. In what condition was mankind originally created?

    _____

3. What brought about mankind's fall? _____

4. Are mankind's problems outward or inward? _____

5. What caused all of mankind's problems? _____

6. Will education and improved living conditions answer all of mankind's problems? _____

    *   Why or why not? _____

        _____

        _____

        _____

Verses to Memorize

*   Romans 5:12
*   1 Corinthians 15:22
*   Jeremiah 17:9

6

SATAN: ANGELOLOGY

Our society depicts Satan or the devil in many ways. Sometimes he appears as a horned monster. Sometimes he's just a trickster in a red suit. The Bible paints a different picture, that of a fallen angel of light, a creature once called Lucifer.

Who is Satan anyway? Is he a person or an influence?

SATAN BEFORE THE FALL

Turn to Ezekiel 28:12–19 and Isaiah 14:12–17.

His Origin

- What does Ezekiel 28:13–15 tell us about the origin of this being? _____
  _____

His Appearance

- What did he look like? _____
  _____

His Name

- In Isaiah 14:12, what is he called? _____
  _____

- In Ezekiel 28:14, he is also called _____
  _____

His Position

Verses 14 and 15 of Ezekiel 28 also tell us that he was perfect, or blameless, the highest ranking creature in God's creation. He was the angel nearest the throne of God. He praised God continually, in all his beauty.

SATAN'S SIN

- Read Isaiah 14:12–14 and describe in your own words what happened to Satan, and why. _____

  _____

  _____

  _____

  _____

  _____

We now know that Satan was created, that he was the greatest among God's creation, that he revolted against God, and that he was cast out of heaven.

- Now, 2 Corinthians 11:14 tells us that Satan is an

  _____

> ### Where is Satan now? In Hell?

- Turn to Job 1:6–7. Here we see Satan coming before God and God asks him to say where he came from. What did Satan say? _____

  _____

- Read Ephesians 2:2; John 12:31; 14:30. What is Satan called in these passages? _____

> ### What is he doing on Earth?

Look up the following Scriptures and fill in what Satan is now doing as prince of this world.

- Zechariah 3:1; 1 Thessalonians. 2:18 _____

  _____

- Matthew 13:19; 2 Corinthians 4:4 _____

  _____

  _____

- John 8:44 _____

  _____

- 2 Corinthians 11:14_____

  _____

- 2 Thessalonians 2:9 _____

  _____

- 1 Peter 5:8 _____

  _____

- Revelation 12:9 _____

  _____

OVERCOMING SATAN

Satan is a very powerful individual. Although he isn't nearly as powerful as God, he is much too strong for you and me. Satan also has followers who do his bidding—followers we will examine in the next chapter. There's only one way to overcome Satan.

- Note 1 Peter 5:8–9. We must be _____ and _____.
  We must _____ in the faith.
  God alone can defeat Satan, and we must stay rooted in His Word.

> *But Satan seems to be winning, and God seems to be losing!*

- Turn to Revelation 20:10. State in your words what the Lord will finally do with Satan. _____

  _____

  _____

1. Where did Satan come from? _____
_____

2. What was he like before he fell into sin? _____
_____
_____

3. What was Satan's purpose before his fall? _____
_____

4. In what way did Satan sin? _____
_____

5. What happened to Satan as a result of sin? _____
_____

6. What is Satan doing now?_____
_____
_____

7. How should we treat the devil today?_____
_____

8. What is his final destiny? _____

Verses to Memorize

- 1 Peter 5:8–9

7

DEMONS: DEMONOLOGY

We have just seen that Satan is a created being. This means that he exists under the permission of God. It also means that, unlike God, he is not all-powerful, he does not know everything, and he cannot be all places at once.

You may be thinking, "But it seems that Satan is in every city and country in the world. If he can't be everywhere at once, who causes all this evil?"

- Turn to Revelation 12:7–9. This passage refers to Satan's fall from heaven. Note the last part of verse 9. What does this tell us about his fall? _____

_____

These angels—how many we do not know—became what the Bible calls demons, or devils (James 2:19; Rev. 9:20).

What are demons like?

- Read Matthew 8:16 and Revelation 16:14. Here these fallen angels are called _____

- What does Luke 24:39 tell us about spirits? _____

_____

We also know that even though demons are spirits, they are personalities who possess feelings and have wills of their own.

- Describe the action of the demons in Acts 19:13–16.

_____

_____

Remember: Since demons are spirits, they cannot be seen by humans, but they are still just as real as if they were visible.

- Read Ephesians 6:11–12. According to this passage we see that Christians face more than just a single deceiver. We are in a warfare against _____

_____

- What kind of beings do you believe this verse is talking about? _____

_____

These are real beings who have personalities, feelings, power, mobility, and intelligence. Have you ever tried to fight someone you could not see? How could you possibly win that fight? We must be able to see what demons do and how they act in order to recognize them!

THE WORK OF DEMONS

- Read 1 Timothy 4:1–2. Here demons are characterized as being deceivers, or seducers. What does this mean?

  _____

  _____

- So in the last days, according to these verses, demons will do what to mankind? _____

  _____

  _____

- Read 2 Corinthians 11:12–15. According to verse 13, what do some human teachers do?_____

  _____

  _____

  _____

- This behavior mimics their true master, Satan. What does he disguise himself as? _____

  _____

According to these verses, some will hear and believe false teaching that is promoted by demons and people somehow under the influence of Satan. Not every person who talks about the Bible and about Jesus Christ is a true teacher.

- Turn to 1 John 4:1–3. Are we to believe every spirit—
  that is, every preacher? _____
  Why? _____

- What is the test of a true minister and a false one?
  _____
  _____
  _____

A word of explanation: 1 John 4:2–3 is talking about more than just the fact that true ministers believe that Jesus came to the earth. Even Satan's ministers will admit that Jesus was a human being who was on this earth 2,000 years ago. What they will not teach, however, is that this same Jesus is God Himself. They may say He was like God or He came from God, but they do not want others to acknowledge His deity.

We must therefore be wary of those who emphasize Christ's humanity to the point of denying His deity. He was both fully God and fully human. He did hunger, tire, and weep, but He did so willingly for our sake.

- Note 1 John 2:22. What does God call a man who denies that Jesus (the person) is the Christ (God in the flesh)?
  _____

- Read 1 John 4:13–15. Do you think a Christian can be indwelled by a demon? _____
  Why? _____
  _____
  _____
  _____

But while we are protected from direct influence, we should not fall prey to false philosophies and teaching that can corrupt our thinking.

- Read 1 Thessalonians 5:22. What are we told to do in this passage? _____
  _____
  _____

- In your own words, what does that verse mean?
  _____
  _____
  _____

- Demons can involve themselves in many things which Christians should avoid. Note Deuteronomy 18:9–11 and list those things which God considers abominations.
  _____
  _____
  _____

- Match the following present day practices to the related abomination listed above.

  - Astrology_____
  - Ouija Boards, Tarot Cards _____
  - Palm Reader _____
  - Talking to the Dead _____

- Should Christians be involved in such things? _____

- Do we need to consult these for guidance? _____

- Where can Christians go for guidance and enlightenment to make decisions and plans? _____
  _____
  _____

> ## *If demons have so much power,*
> ## *how can we ever defeat them?*

- Turn back to Ephesians 6:12. Now read verses 13–17 and especially note verses 16–17. What does Paul say we're to use to defeat Satan and his forces?

  1. _____
  2. _____
  3. _____

Are you really using God's weapons in this battle against your spiritual enemies, or are you trying to win the battle your own way? Maybe you've decided by now that you just can't win—you've already quit! Maybe right now you're fooling around with those things you listed earlier. Remember, you are kept by the power of God. Isn't He able to keep you from these things, if you will only ask Him? Stay close to the Lord. Only He can keep us true and faithful.

> ## *Are drugs a gateway for demonic influence?*

- Read Revelation 9:21; 18:23; 21:8; and 22:15. What one sin is mentioned in all four of these passages?

  _____

- This phrase is translated from the Greek word *pharmakeia*, from which we get *pharmacy* and *pharmaceuticals*. In biblical times, sorcery and drug use were closely related. People would seek otherworldly experiences through the use of crude hallucinogens. Note Isaiah 47:9 and Acts 8:9. According to Acts 8:9, what was Simon doing with drugs? _____

  _____
  _____

- Should a Christian therefore get involved in the misuse of drugs? _____

Why? _____
_____
_____

1. What were demons originally? _____

2. How did they become demons? _____
    _____

3. Describe the appearance of demons. _____
    _____

4. Name at least two things that demons do to obscure the
    truth. _____
    _____

5. How can you tell a true minister from a false one?
    _____
    _____
    _____

6. Name some of the activities in which demons can be
    involved today. _____
    _____
    _____

7. What three things does Paul say we are to use to defeat
    Satan and his forces? _____
    _____
    _____
    _____

Verses to Memorize

• Ephesians 6:10–12

8

THE SECOND COMING: ESCHATOLOGY

Although this is the last chapter of the *Meat* booklet, it is certainly not the least important. It may just be the most encouraging for you, for we are now going to read what the Bible says about the second coming of the Lord Jesus Christ. For those who have accepted Him, it is thrilling to know that one day He will return to Earth.

Maybe you've heard someone say something like this, "Everybody is always talking about Jesus coming. They've been saying that for hundreds of years, and He still hasn't come. I say it's a big joke." The Bible talks about that kind of person. Read 2 Peter 3:3–4.

But how do I know that Jesus really will return some day?

- Turn to Acts 1:8–11. Who is speaking in verse 8?

  _____

- To whom is He saying these things? _____

- What happened after He said these things?

  _____

  _____

- In verse 11, how did the angels say Christ would return to Earth? _____

  _____

  _____

- So if Jesus' physical body ascended to the sky when He left, how do you believe He will return?

  _____

  _____

  _____

But will He come in the air or return to Earth?

TWO PARTS OF HIS SECOND COMING

Keep in mind that Christ's second coming is in two parts. First He will come in the air, and later He will return to the earth.

The Rapture

- Turn to 1 Thessalonians 4:16–17, and read very carefully. Who are people called the dead in Christ?

  _____

- When will they rise from the dead? _____

  _____

- What will happen to the living Christians? _____

  _____

- According to verse 17, Where will these two groups meet the Lord? _____

This part of Christ's return is called the Rapture of the Church. The word _rapture_ comes from the Latin _rapiemur_, which is how the Vulgate, a 4th century Latin version of the Bible, translated the original Greek word _harpadzo_, which means "caught up suddenly."

Will the unsaved go up as well?

- Read 1 Thessalonians 4:16 again. Who will rise first?

  _____

- Not just the dead, but the dead in Christ. What does that mean? _____

  _____

If only the dead in Christ arise, what happens to the dead who are not in Christ? Where are they when all of this happens? What happens to them?

- Read Luke 16:22–23 and answer the above questions by noting where the rich man was. _____

_____

Since the dead in Christ go up at the Rapture while the dead out of Christ stay in hell at the Rapture, we can draw some conclusions concerning those who are alive at the Rapture.

- Again, from 1 Thessalonians 4:17, what will happen to the living Christians when the Rapture takes place?

_____

_____

- What can we assume happens to those who are alive at the Rapture, but have not accepted Christ?

_____

_____

_____

How could someone survive being caught up like this?

- Read 1 Corinthians 15:51–53. According to these verses what will happen to all Christians' bodies?

_____

_____

- What does it mean to put on immortality?

_____

_____

A few basic facts about the Rapture:

- According to Matthew 24:44, when will it occur?

_____

- Read John 14:3 and 1 Thessalonians 4:16–17. Who will be involved? _____

_____

_____

- And according to 1 Thessalonians 4:17, where will we meet Christ? _____

_____

> ### What will happen to those left on Earth?

- They will endure seven horrible years known as the Tribulation. Matthew 24:21–22 describes that period of time. What will it be like? _____

_____

_____

_____

According to 2 Thessalonians 2:6–7, the Holy Spirit will not restrain the work of evil during this period. Satan will be allowed more opportunities to work openly. Sin will completely prevail and God will pour out His wrath. This is a time of terrible judgment, when good and evil will be crystal clear for those left on Earth.

Match the passage with the event that will occur.

	1. Terrible sores upon men	A. Revelation 16:2
	2. Men scorched with the sun	B. Revelation 16:3
	3. Sea turned to blood	C. Revelation 16:4
	4. Darkness on the earth	D. Revelation 16:8
	5. Rivers turned to blood	E. Revelation 16:10
	6. Terrible earthquakes	F. Revelation 16:17–20
	7. 90 lb. hailstones	G. Revelation 16:21

> ### What will happen when Christ finally comes back to Earth?

Keep in mind that Christ will first come in the air (the Rapture) and will take all the saved, both dead and alive, to be with Him in heaven. Those who are left will endure seven horrible years of judgment (the Tribulation), after which the Lord will then return to Earth (the Revelation).

- Now note what will happen. Read Matthew 24:30–31; Luke 21:27. Who will see Christ coming? Remember who will be on Earth at that time. _____

  _____

  _____

- What will they do when they see Him coming? _____

  _____

- Keep verse 31 in mind. Read Jude 14 and Zechariah 14:5. Who will come with the Lord at this time?

  _____

- According to Zechariah 14:4, where exactly will Christ return? _____

  _____

- And in Revelation 20:1–3, what will happen to Satan?

  _____

  _____

For 1,000 years, Christ and His saints will live and rule on the Earth. This is called the Millennial Reign of Christ.

- Now read Revelation 20:7–10 and state in your own words what will happen. _____

  _____

  _____

  _____

- Read Revelation 20:11–15. State in your own words what will happen. _____

_____

_____

_____

_____

What a sad and terrible day for those who have never trusted Christ. They must then spend eternity, forever burning, in the Lake of Fire. How tragic!

- But in Revelation 21:1–6, what does the Bible say that God has prepared for those who accepted Christ? _____

_____

_____

_____

_____

Complete This Section Without Looking Back at the Lesson

1. Define the following terms as to what they represent in future world events:

   - The Rapture _____

   _____

   - The Tribulation _____

   _____

   - The Millennial Reign _____

   _____

   - The Revelation _____

   _____

2. Put each of these four events in their proper order of occurrence. _____

   _____

3. What are the two aspects of the second coming of Christ?

   _____

   _____

4. Who will be caught up in the Rapture? _____

   _____

5. Explain what happens to our bodies at the Rapture and give a verse to prove your statement. _____

   _____

   _____

   _____

6. Name at least three differences between the Rapture and the Revelation of Christ: _____

   _____

   _____

   _____

   _____

7. What will be the final abode of the unsaved? Give a verse to prove your answer. _____

   _____

   _____

Verses to Memorize

- Acts 1:11
- 1 Thessalonians 4:16–17

EXAMINATION QUESTIONS

Complete the following questions without looking back in your book for answers.

1. What does the word *inspiration* mean?_____
   _____

2. Name four ways we can know that the Bible is the inspired Word of God. _____
   _____
   _____
   _____

3. Name the two types of inspiration._____
   _____
   _____

4. Write 2 Timothy 3:16 from memory. _____
   _____
   _____
   _____

5. What do we mean when we speak of the deity of Jesus Christ?_____
   _____

6. List three names of Christ that prove He is God.
   _____
   _____

7. Write John 20:28–29 from memory. _____
   _____
   _____
   _____
   _____

8. Give a simple definition of the Trinity. _____
   _____
   _____

9. Name three major proofs of the Trinity.
   _____
   _____
   _____

10. What four great truths must we discard if we reject the doctrine of the Trinity? _____

_____

_____

_____

11. List two verses that present the Holy Spirit as a person.

_____

_____

12. List four words that describe the work of the Holy Spirit and describe what each means.

_____

_____

_____

_____

13. State when each of the following happens:

- The new birth _____
- The baptism of the Spirit _____
- The indwelling of the Spirit _____
- The filling of the Spirit _____

14. Write 1 Corinthians 6:19–20 from memory.

_____

_____

_____

_____

_____

_____

15. Name the four areas affected by Adam's sin.

_____

_____

_____

_____

16. What brought about man's fall? _____

17. Are man's problems outward or inward? _____
    How do you know? _____
    _____

18. What is the only true cure for man's problems?
    _____

19. What was Satan like before he sinned?
    _____
    _____

20. In what way did Satan sin? Give a reference.
    _____
    _____

21. What is Satan doing now? _____
    _____
    _____

22. How should we treat the devil today?_____
    _____

23. Write 1 Peter 5:8–9 from memory. _____
    _____
    _____
    _____
    _____

24. Where did demons come from? _____
    _____

25. How can you tell a true minister from a false one?
    _____
    _____
    _____

26. Name three things Paul says we are to use to defeat Satan
    and his forces. _____
    _____
    _____

27. Explain what will happen during each of the following:

- The Rapture_____

  _____

- The Tribulation _____

  _____

- The Revelation _____

  _____

28. What are the two aspects of the second coming of Christ?

  _____

  _____

  _____

29. Name at least three differences between the Rapture and the Revelation of Christ. _____

  _____

  _____

  _____

  _____

30. Each doctrine studied in this booklet goes by a theological term that is listed with the title of each chapter. List each chapter and its theological name. We have listed the first title for you.

- The Inspiration of the Bible: Bibliology

- _____

- _____

- _____

- _____

- _____

- _____

- _____

31. Give one verse that teaches each of the following doctrines:

- The inspiration of the Bible _____

- The Deity of Jesus Christ _____

- That God the Father, Son, and Holy Spirit are three, yet one God _____

- That man is a sinner and must die _____

- That Christ is coming back _____